Railway Elegance

'Ripening wheat heralds the approach of harvest-time'.
On a hot afternoon in late July, a 'Peak' emerges from the darkness of Wickwar Tunnel into
bright summer sunshine with the Etruria-St. Blazey clay empties.   29 July 1978.

Diverted from her normal route to run via the 'Berks and Hants' line, the 09.15 Paddington to Swansea, hauled by Class 47 No. 47496, finds herself keeping close company with the Kennet and Avon canal as she sweeps past the attractive small village of Little Bedwyn.
7 September 1975.

Railway Elegance

WESTERN REGION TRAINS IN THE ENGLISH COUNTRYSIDE

IVO PETERS

Oxford Publishing Company

'The driver's view'.
A picture taken from the cab of Class 50 No. 50050 hauling the 09.45 ex-Paddington, as she meets a sister Class 50 heading east with an up express.   13 June 1974.

First published in the U.K. 1985 by Oxford Publishing Co., Link House, West Street, Poole, Dorset, BH15 1LL.

Copyright © 1985 Ivo Peters and Oxford Publishing Co.

British Library Cataloguing in Publication Data.

Peters, Ivo
    Railway elegance.
    1. British Rail. *Western Region* — History — Pictorial works 1/1 2. Diesel locomotives — England — History — Pictorial works
    I. Title
    625.2'66'0942 1/1 TJ619

ISBN 0 7137 1479 4

Colour origination by Colthouse Repro Ltd, Bournemouth.
Typeset by Weaver & Associates, Weymouth, Dorset.
Printed in Spain by Printer Industria Gráfica s.a. Barcelona D.L.B. 6045-1985

All colour transparencies appearing within this book were taken on Kodak film; either Ektachrome X, or the later version of this film, Ektachrome 64.

ACKNOWLEDGEMENTS

I wish, in particular, to express my gratitude to the successive Western Divisional Managers for their kindness in granting me, over many years, the privilege of an annual photographic permit, without which many of the pictures in this book would not have been taken.

Several of my friends have helped in the preparation of this book. For their specialized knowledge and advice, I am deeply indebted to Mike Arlett, Peter Pike and Peter Skelton. Once again Peggy Leitch has kindly taken on the task of deciphering my illegible handwriting and typing my manuscript; and, as with all my books, Angela O'Shea has been of immense help with her constructive criticism of my choice of pictures and their arrangement. To all these friends who have given me so much help, I am most grateful.

IVO PETERS
1984

Note for budding railway photographers of today.
    Although, for reasons of safety, British Rail no longer grant photographic permits, several of my favourite pictures in this book were taken from 'the public's side of the fence'.

In the late afternoon, as the heat at last began to fade after a glorious June day, the 16.20 HST from Paddington leaves Twerton Tunnel behind as she accelerates rapidly westwards from Bath on the run over to Temple Meads, Bristol.

HST is the abbreviation for the High Speed Train, British Rail's outstanding technical creation which has revolutionized rail travel in Great Britain.   24 June 1979.

FOREWORD

A railway running through the countryside, with graceful sweeping embankments, attractive bridges, majestic viaducts and artistically designed tunnel mouths, often complements and enhances the beauty of the surrounding scenery. When a train comes into view, few are unable to appreciate the elegance of its progress and the brief noise it makes is not offensive, quickly dying away as the train disappears in the distance.

How different has been the impact on our land of the advance of the modern motorway. Great swathes of concrete, cut imperiously straight through the countryside, scar the scenery far and wide, and the hordes of road vehicles flowing restlessly to and fro in a seemingly never-ending stream, destroy utterly the peace and serenity of the surrounding fields and woods.

Ivo Peters, born in the small village of Corston in Somerset, has always loved the countryside. At a very early age he also became fascinated by the railway, and so began his life-long love of trains.

A dedicated amateur railway photographer for fifty-six years, he photographed the railway scene far and wide. But nothing gave Ivo greater pleasure than taking pictures of trains in the countryside, when his endeavour was always to try and show how the elegance of the train blended in with the beauty of the surroundings.

P. S. G. Witter,
Divisional Manager,
British Rail,
Bristol.

THE FOUR SEASONS — SPRING

On a bright spring morning in early May, an up express from Bristol to Paddington, hauled by a Brush Type 4, heads east beneath the cherry blossom in Sydney Gardens, Bath.
5 May 1970.

SUMMER

In the early evening of a perfect summer's day, a Class 50 passes by a field of buttercups as she ambles through the Wiltshire countryside with a westbound goods train. 3 June 1980.

AUTUMN

The Limpley Stoke valley on a fresh November day — with a definite autumn 'nip' in the air. Brush Type 4 No. D1598, still in the old two-tone green livery, runs beside the River Avon as she hauls an eastbound goods through the valley towards the Dundas Aqueduct.

5 November 1970.

WINTER

The 10.50 HST, Bristol, Temple Meads, to Paddington leaves behind a trail of swirling snow as, travelling very fast, she draws near to Middle Hill Tunnel, Box.   24 January 1979.

'Western' Class diesel-hydraulic No. D1052 *Western Viceroy*, in charge of a down special, approaches Knighton Crossing, east of Swindon. 7 October 1971.

WESTERN REGION MOTIVE POWER CONTROVERSY DIESEL-HYDRAULIC

When British Railways ordained that diesel power was to replace the steam locomotive, the Western Region, following in the tradition of the old Great Western Railway, decided 'to go their own way'. Whilst all the other Regions of BR chose the diesel-electric system, the Western Region decided to adopt the principle of diesel-hydraulic traction

'Warship' Class diesel-hydraulic No. D810 *Cockade*, running west through Sydney Gardens, Bath, with a down goods. 28 July 1972.

Diesel-electric Class 47 No. 47493, on a down express from Paddington, heading west from Middle Hill Tunnel, Box.
6 May 1975.

— OR DIESEL-ELECTRIC?

which had several significant advantages over the diesel-electric, and was proving so successful in West Germany. But the 'official opposition' was too great, and the Western's bold move was to end in ultimate defeat, with the diesel-electric system finally 'winning the day'.

A pair of diesel-electric Class 31 locomotives, running light-engine down the West of England main line, draw near to Frome.
26 May 1978.

INTERESTING VISITORS TO THE WESTERN REGION

Two over-gilded lilies?
A pair of 'spruced-up' Eastern Region Class 31s, heading north-west through the Limpley Stoke valley with an enthusiasts' special.   22 October 1977.

Eastern Region Deltic, No. 55003 *Meld*, making full use of her 3,300 bhp, climbs rapidly away eastwards from the Severn Tunnel with her enthusiasts' special.   12 October 1975.

Two Class 40s, Nos. 40081 and 40084, making a cautious approach to Westbury with a special from London.   9 October 1977.

THE EVOLUTION OF THE HIGH SPEED TRAIN (HST)

The 'Blue Pullman' — the forerunner to the HST in comfort, speed and silence — began running on the Western Region in 1960.

Test running over the Western Region of the prototype HST commenced in late 1974 and the production version entered service in 1976.

The 'Blue Pullman' setting off through Sydney Gardens, Bath, on the morning run up to Paddington.   2 May 1968.

The prototype HST nearing Middle Hill Tunnel, Box, with an up working from Bristol, Temple Meads, to Paddington.   7 July 1975.

A Western Region HST (7 cars and 2 power cars) running east through the Limpley Stoke valley on a Sunday diversion up to London. The train is the 07.35 Swansea to Paddington. 2 November 1980.

TWERTON TUNNEL, BATH — THE WESTERN END

The portals at both ends of this tunnel were most attractively designed, little castellated turrets adorning the sides of the high-arched tunnel mouths.

◄ Brush Type 4 No. D1944, still in the two-tone green livery, emerges from the west end of Twerton Tunnel with a train from Salisbury. (I disclaim any connection with the train's reporting number!)

In 1969 BR embarked on a major classification scheme for all their diesel locomotives. The Brush Type 4s became Class 47. However, the subsequent re-numbering of BR's fleet of diesel locomotives did not really get into its stride until 1974.   16 July 1971.

A diesel-hydraulic 'Hymek' — still in the attractive two-tone green livery — heading west from the tunnel with the afternoon train from Portsmouth Harbour to Cardiff. ▶
15 July 1971.

On a run from Bath over to Bristol — the special HST (4 cars, 2 power cars) assembled for Her Majesty the Queen's use during her Silver Jubilee visit to the Bath/Bristol area. The HST chosen for this duty was, appropriately, No. 253025.   8 August 1977.

TWERTON TUNNEL, BATH — THE EASTERN END

A 'Peak' in charge of an up goods, leaves the tunnel behind as she heads towards Bath at a much more sedate pace. ▶
17 May 1978

An up HST — the 10.50 Bristol to Paddington — travelling very fast, emerges from the east end of Twerton Tunnel.
17 August 1978.

THE ENCHANTMENT OF BATH SPA STATION AT NIGHT

The 18.48 (Fridays only) from Paddington, hauled by a Class 50, about to set off from Bath for the run over to Bristol, Temple Meads. 7 March 1980.

An SR Class 33 arrives with an evening train from Portsmouth.

5 September 1980.

The 19.20 HST from Paddington waiting in Bath Station after arriving two minutes early. This HST — No. 253031 — had only recently entered service, being one of a new batch powered by GEC traction motors.

7 March 1980.

CROSSING OVER THE RIVER AVON EAST OF BATH STATION

Class 47 No. 47478 with a down express, slowing for the stop at Bath, crosses over the River Avon just to the east of Bath Station. The magnificent steeple in the background is that of St. John's Church, South Parade, Bath.

15 September 1975.

A 'Peak' in charge of a down ballast train, has just passed under Brunel's iron footbridge, as she runs through Sydney Gardens, Bath.

6 May 1979.

THE EASTERN APPROACH TO BATH THROUGH SYDNEY GARDENS

When Brunel planned the route for the Great Western Railway, he arranged for the eastern approach to Bath to pass through Sydney Gardens. Since the line was built, over 140 years ago, hardly anything has changed. The high retaining walls on the right, and the ornate iron footbridge over the line are just as Brunel built them.

After the stop at Bath Station, the 11.15 from Bristol to Paddington, hauled by a Class 47 and a Class 50, gathers speed through Sydney Gardens on the resumption of the journey up to London.   7 May 1975.

SYDNEY GARDENS, BATH   In early May, the trees in Sydney Gardens are really superb.

Maytime in Sydney Gardens. The tail end of an up HST accelerating away from Bath for the run up to Paddington.

4 May 1980.

PASSING BENEATH THE CHERRY BLOSSOM IN SYDNEY GARDENS

A 'Western' Class diesel-hydraulic, No. D1071 *Western Renown* passes beneath the cherry blossom as she heads away east from Bath with an up parcels train.   26 April 1973.

The 12.45 from Paddington, hauled by Brush Type 4 No. D1945, coasts quietly into view round the curve and under the cherry blossom. She was already slowing down in preparation for her scheduled stop at Bath.   2 May 1973.

Whilst waiting in the up loop at Bathampton, an HST engaged on the Bath-Bristol 'shuttle' service, is passed by a Diesel Multiple Unit (DMU) on a local service over from Westbury.　　　　13 May 1977.

BATHAMPTON

An HST, after waiting in the up loop, crosses over on to the down line and returns to Bath for the run back to Bristol.
13 May 1977.

Due to the London main line via Bath being closed because of a major land slip near Dauntsey, HSTs ran a 'shuttle' service between Bath and Bristol for the benefit of Bath passengers wishing to travel to London. The Bristol-London main line via Badminton was unaffected.

The middle roads through Bath Station having been lifted, it was not possible to stable the 'shuttle' HSTs at Bath in between trips, so they had to run empty out to Bathampton, and wait there in the up loop until it was time to come back to Bath for the return trip over to Bristol.

CROSSING OVER THE RIVER AVON AT BATHFORD

A down HST — the 11.20 from Paddington — crosses the bridge over the River Avon at Bathford.
21 September 1978.

Two Class 37s pass by, heading west with an empty stone train. In the foreground is the site of the now vanished Box goods yard.
28 August 1975.

GHOSTS OF THE PAST

THE SITE OF BOX STATION AND GOODS YARD, NOW — WITH EVERYTHING GONE — ONLY THE MEMORY REMAINS

A Class 31 on an up parcels train, running east from the spot where Box Station used to be.
23 October 1978.

Falcon emerges from Middle Hill Tunnel, Box, with the 10.45 express from Paddington to Bristol, Temple Meads.   14 July 1972.

PROTOTYPE DIESEL

BR having decided to eliminate steam traction completely, drew up specifications for a series of standard diesel-electric locomotives of varying horse power. Several locomotive manufacturers built prototypes for consideration by BR. A contender for the Type 4 specification was Co-Co *Falcon*, built by Brush. During the period of trial running, she remained the property of the manufacturers, and carried the number D0280. At the conclusion of the tests, *Falcon* was taken into BR stock and given the number 1200.

MEMORIES REVIVED — 'The Severn Valley Limited', a special train from Bridgnorth to London arranged by the Severn Valley Railway and composed of ten of their privately preserved GWR coaches in 'chocolate and cream' livery, draws near to Middle Hill Tunnel, Box. BR of course, provided the motive power, a Class 47 diesel-electric locomotive, No. 47120.   13 November 1976.

AND THE MODERN
SCENE

An up express hauled by a Class 50, nearing Middle Hill Tunnel, Box.   13 November 1976.

A down HST, running west from Middle Hill Tunnel, sweeps past at very high speed.

13 November 1976.

AUTUMN APPROACH TO MIDDLE HILL TUNNEL, BOX

An up HST — the 10.45 from Weston-super-Mare to Paddington — about to enter Middle Hill Tunnel, Box, in the late autumn of 1980.   12 November 1980.

THE WESTERN PORTAL OF MIDDLE HILL TUNNEL, BOX

The design of both portals of Middle Hill Tunnel, and the western end portal of Box Tunnel, are most attractive. They were made very tall, to give the appearance of great space inside so as to reassure travellers in the early days. However, once inside, and in the dark, the tunnels come down to normal dimensions:

The 13.20 down HST from Paddington, bursts out of the tunnel, heading swiftly towards Bath.
1 June 1977.

THE EASTERN END OF MIDDLE HILL TUNNEL

The 10.15 up express from Bristol, Temple Meads, hauled by a Class 47, emerging from the attractive eastern portal of Middle Hill Tunnel, Box.   16 May 1973

A Class 50 on an up express, darts out of the tunnel as she heads eastwards on the run up to Paddington. 2 September 1976.

The prototype HST, on an early morning run from Bristol up to Paddington, leaves Middle Hill Tunnel behind. 20 May 1975.

BETWEEN BOX AND MIDDLE HILL TUNNELS

The 10.45 down express from Paddington, Class 47 hauled, running swiftly from Box Tunnel towards Middle Hill Tunnel.
28 July 1972.

With the summer evening shadows lengthening, the 17.20 HST from Paddington emerges at high speed.
18 June 1978.

BOX TUNNEL

Through Box Tunnel, which is almost two miles long and dead straight, the line climbs eastwards at 1 in 100. Apart from this climb, and a similar incline eastwards at Dauntsey, such was the brilliance of Brunel, that the line which he planned and built for the Great Western Railway to link London with Bristol, via Bath, is virtually level throughout.

For very many years there has been a legend that the rising sun may be seen shining right through the tunnel on just one day in the year, 9th April, Brunel's birthday. Disappointingly, this is not so. Standing at the western end it is possible — if the weather is kind — to see the sun shining straight through the tunnel on just three days of the year, but the dates are 15-17 April; and because of the rising gradient of 1 in 100, the time is about half an hour after sunrise.

THE LIMPLEY STOKE VALLEY

An up Sunday HST, diverted to run over the 'Berks and Hants' line, enters the northern end of the very lovely Limpley Stoke valley.

24 September 1978.

For the next four miles, the railway shares this beautiful valley with the River Avon and the Kennet and Avon Canal.

SUNDAY EXCURSION   Class 47 No. 47086, running beside the river, heads south-east in charge of a Sunday 'Mystery' Excursion from Swansea. (Was the destination Weymouth?)   28 May 1978.

PASSING CLAVERTON WEIR

A refurbished Diesel Multiple Unit passes Claverton Weir in the early morning as it runs towards Bathampton.
15 May 1979.

NEAR CLAVERTON

In mid-afternoon, the 14.07 Portsmouth Harbour to Bristol, Temple Meads, express, passes by, hauled by SR Class 33 No. 33021.
16 May 1980.

RUNNING THROUGH THE LIMPLEY STOKE VALLEY BESIDE THE RIVER AVON

With the placid River Avon in the foreground, a Sunday diversion express from Plymouth to Edinburgh heads towards Bathampton, behind a Class 47.

11 May 1980.

The Sunday morning 09.59 from Bristol, Temple Meads to Portsmouth Harbour, hauled by Class 31 No. 31421, running south-east, towards Limpley Stoke.   11 May 1980.

A Sunday HST from Paddington to Bristol, diverted to come down the 'Berks & Hants' line running through the Limpley Stoke valley towards Bathampton.   27 August 1978.

DIVERTED TRAFFIC

From Reading westwards, the Western Region has two routes to the West of England. The original main line runs via Swindon, Bath and Bristol down to Taunton, where it is met by the other, newer, line which has come down the 'Berks & Hants' line to Westbury, and then on via Castle Cary to Taunton. The cross-country line from Bathampton, down through the Limpley Stoke valley, to Westbury, links the two routes. This link is very useful, particularly at week-ends, when one of the routes may be closed for engineering work, and all traffic is then diverted to run over the other main line.

THE CARDIFF-PORTSMOUTH SERVICE

On a bright but chilly day in late March, the morning Cardiff-Portsmouth express heads south-east hauled by a diesel-hydraulic 'Hymek'.　　　20 March 1972.

Eight years later, after the 'Hymeks' had been superseded by diesel-electrics, an SR Class 33 runs north-west with a Portsmouth-Cardiff express.

11 May 1980.

Early on an overcast August morning, the Royal train — which had been stabled overnight near Bradford Junction — glides sedately north from Limpley Stoke towards the Dundas Aqueduct. In charge of the train is an immaculate 'Western' diesel-hydraulic, No. D1058 *Western Nobleman*.
9 August 1973.

THE ROYAL TRAIN

In 1973 the Royal train was still largely composed of very elegant but elderly coaches. Sadly, these were no longer painted in the gorgeous, old LNWR 'plum and split-milk' livery so beloved by King George V that, when the LMS was formed, he insisted on the livery of the Royal train remaining unchanged. Today, all the old coaches have been replaced with modern stock.

An express, running south-east, passes by the attractive small village of Claverton.
24 March 1972.

PASSING THE VILLAGE OF CLAVERTON

The imposing mansion set high up the side of the valley, above the village, is the city of Bath's American Museum.

TWO PICTURES TAKEN IN THE AUTUMN FROM THE DUNDAS AQUEDUCT

The 11.30 Sunday Bristol to Paddington HST, diverted to run via the 'Berks & Hants' line, about to pass beneath the Dundas Aqueduct which carries the Kennet and Avon Canal over both the railway and the River Avon.   2 November 1980.

A southbound goods trundles leisurely through the valley, hauled by a Class 47, No. 47091.   8 November 1978.

FRESHFORD

A Class 31, in charge of a southbound local, about to stop at Freshford Station. 29 April 1977.

An engineers' train, hauled by a 'Peak', draws near to Freshford. 20 August 1978.

NEARING AVONCLIFF

Diesel-hydraulic 'Warship', No. D847, *Strongbow,* draws near to Avoncliff with a long train of empty coal wagons from Portishead Power Station, bound for the collieries at Radstock. 5 November 1970.

On a bright winter's morning in mid-December, the 09.50, Sunday HST from Paddington, diverted to run down the 'Berks & Hants' line, heads north-west towards Freshford. 17 December 1978.

RUNNING BESIDE THE RIVER WEST OF BRADFORD-ON-AVON

An afternoon goods, hauled by two Class 47s, runs beside the river as she draws near to Avoncliff. 28 July 1978.

An eastbound express, in the charge of Class 47, No. 47113, leaves 'The Avenue' behind as she approaches Bradford-on-Avon.
4 September 1977.

'THE AVENUE'

As the railway draws near to Bradford-on-Avon, the line is bordered on both sides by tall, stately trees. This is a beautiful setting and is known locally as 'The Avenue'.

A WINTERY APPROACH TO BRADFORD-ON-AVON

On a frosty November morning, diesel-hydraulic 'Hymek' No. D7005, in two-tone green livery, nears Bradford-on-Avon with the 09.15 Cardiff to Portsmouth Harbour train.
11 November 1971.

And the same spot two years later. A short parcels train trundles by, heading towards Bradford-on-Avon. The locomotive is a diesel-electric Brush Type 2, No. D5827 — still in the old livery — her now rather worn paintwork contrasting sharply with the beautiful autumn colouring of the trees in the background.

When BR carried out their major classification scheme for all diesel locomotives, the Brush Type 2s became Class 31.   5 November 1973.

CROSSING OVER THE RIVER AT BRADFORD-ON-AVON

Appearing quietly from behind the trees, a diesel-hydraulic Hymek, in blue livery, passes over the River Avon with the 09.07 Cardiff to Portsmouth Harbour.

27 April 1973.

With the sound of her approach drowned by the roar of the weir, Brush Type 4 No. D1689 suddenly appeared, heading towards Bradford-on-Avon with the 09.42 Weymouth to Bristol, Temple Meads. 27 April 1973.

Signalman Mervyn Halbrook on duty in the signal box. 14 August 1973.

BRADFORD JUNCTION

There are, in fact, three junctions here, but all come under the one title, 'Bradford Junction'. A single line which leaves the London-Bristol main line two miles west of Chippenham at Thingley Junction, comes down through Melksham to join the Bathampton-Westbury line. However, just before so doing, it splits — at the North Junction — to make two connections, one heading towards Bathampton and the other towards Westbury.

Mervyn Halbrook taking the single-line
tablet from the driver of Brush Type 4 No.
D1728, which had come down from
Thingley Junction with the 08.00 Swindon-
Westbury goods.　　　　14 August 1973.

After giving up the token at the signalbox, a
Hymek, with a short military train from
Chippenham to Warminster, runs towards
the South Junction.　　　3 November 1971.

▲
Two Brush Type 4s, Nos. D1602 and D1604, in charge of an empty ballast train, having come down from Thingley, pass over the North Junction on to the East Chord for the run back to Bristol.

2 September 1973.

BRADFORD JUNCTION — THE NORTH JUNCTION AND EAST CHORD

A Class 25, No. 25157, standing on the East Chord with an engineers' train.

17 June 1975.

THE EAST CHORD

On a cold but bright Sunday morning in mid-April, the engineers had possession of the up main line between Bathampton and Thingley Junctions, and all Bristol-London trains routed through Bath, were diverted to run via Bradford Junction. Having come down the Limpley Stoke valley, and through Bradford-on-Avon, Brush Type 4 No. D1939 brings the 11.15 ex-Temple Meads, Bristol, gently round the East Chord at Bradford Junction.   15 April 1973.

Class 47 No. 47214, coming round the long curve on the main line, draws near to the South Junction with the 09.05 Cardiff to Weymouth.   17 June 1975.

THE SOUTH JUNCTION

Class 50 No. 50019, in charge of a London-Bristol train which had been diverted down the 'Berks & Hants' line, swings carefully round the curve on the main line at the South Junction. The speed restriction here is 40 mph.   6 July 1975.

THE WEST JUNCTION

As the engineers had complete occupation of Box Tunnel, all traffic from Paddington to Bristol, routed through Bath, was diverted at Thingley Junction to run via Bradford Junction to Bathampton Junction where it rejoined the main line. A down HST, having carefully traversed the East Chord, passes slowly over Bradford West Junction and then the trailing crossover, before accelerating away on the run up to Bathampton.   3 September 1978.

RUNNING SOUTH FROM BRADFORD JUNCTION

A 'Hymek' in charge of the morning Cardiff-Portsmouth train, after negotiating the South Junction, starts to gather speed again on the continuation of the run over to Westbury.
20 July 1971.

A derailment having completely blocked the Bristol-Taunton main line, all traffic normally using this route had to be diverted to run via Bath and Westbury down to Taunton. The 10.25 Manchester to Penzance, hauled by 'Peak' No. D50, was one of the trains affected and is seen here accelerating away from the speed restriction round Bradford South Junction.   13 September 1971.

HAWKERIDGE JUNCTION

This junction was put in during World War Two, to take a line round to Heywood Road Junction on the West of England main line. This formed an East Chord and made a triangular junction layout east of Westbury.

A diverted Bristol-Paddington train, hauled by a Class 47, passes Hawkeridge Junction signal box and enters the East Chord to take her round to Heywood Road Junction, for the run up to Reading over the 'Berks & Hants' line.   16 September 1973.

On a beautiful morning in early October, diesel-hydraulic 'Hymek' No. D7005, still in the original two-tone green livery, heads west from Hawkeridge Junction towards Westbury with a train of empty hopper wagons.   6 October 1971.

After coming down the 'Berks and Hants' line, Class 50 No. 50028, in charge of the 08.15 Paddington-Bristol, Temple Meads, express, comes slowly off the East Chord on to the main line.   29 June 1975.

Class 47 No. 47500, with a diverted Paddington-Bristol train, coming carefully round the East Chord and about to join the main line.   29 June 1975.

On an overcast day in August, an up express for Paddington, hauled by a diesel-hydraulic 'Warship', No. D838, *Rapid*, still in the old red livery, sets off from Westbury. After passing the North Box, the train will take the line out to Heywood Road Junction where it will rejoin the main line for the continuation of the run up to Paddington.   21 August 1970.

WESTBURY

The rail layout here is most interesting. The West of England main line (the 'Berks & Hants') used to run through Westbury Station, but a 'Westbury cut-off' line, by-passing the station' and its severe speed restrictions, was built in the early 1930s. The Junctions at the east and west ends of this 'cut-off' are Heywood Road and Fairwood respectively. Then, coming into Westbury from the north is the line from Bradford Junction, whilst just a little way to the west of the station is the line that sets off in a south-easterly direction for Salisbury.

Western Marquis standing beside the now demolished South Box. This is where the line for
Salisbury curves away south-east from the main line.   30 June 1975.

Earlier in the morning, diesel-hydraulic No. D1046, *Western Marquis*, had come in off the line
from Salisbury with a train of empty stone wagons from Botley.   30 June 1975.

WESTBURY   Diesel-hydraulic No. D1009 *Western Invader*, running in from Fairwood Junction with a train of stone carried in Foster Yeoman's own wagons from their quarry at Merehead.

4 September 1975.

WESTWARD-BOUND FROM WESTBURY

After coming in on the Salisbury line and running round her train, SR Class 33 No. 33005, in charge of a train of petrol tankers from Fawley, sets off again for Fairwood Junction and the West of England main line.   4 September 1975.

Having made the scheduled stop at Westbury Station, Class 47 No. 47472 resumes her journey with her train down to Weymouth.   4 September 1975.

SR Type 3 No. D6539, with a train of ballast for Woking from Whatley Quarry, Frome, bears left at Fairwood Junction on to the line into Westbury. At Westbury she would run round her train and then set off again down the Salisbury line.   22 February 1971.

FAIRWOOD JUNCTION

At the western end of the 'Westbury cut-off' line.

A Class 47 in charge of a down freight, comes round the Westbury cut-off line, towards Fairwood Junction. On the left is the line coming out from Westbury Station, which joins the 'Westbury cut-off' at Fairwood Junction.
17 March 1975.

With a thunderstorm brewing, SR Class 33 No. 33007 sets her tanker train back on to the up road of the cut-off line, to allow a Bristol-Weymouth stopping train to overtake her.
17 March 1975.

FAIRWOOD JUNCTION — Brush Type 4 No. D1723, in charge of the 10.05 Weymouth to Bristol, Temple Meads, swings left on to the line leading into Westbury Station.

6 November 1973.

A 'MEETING' OF 'HYMEKS'

Diesel-hydraulic 'Hymek' No. D7003 — still in the old green livery — comes out from Westbury, and across the Junction, with a train of empty coal wagons bound for the Radstock collieries.   22 February 1971.

Whilst a little later, another 'Hymek', No. D7001, in blue livery, passes Fairwood Junction signal box with the 09.41 up semi-fast from Weymouth.   22 February 1971.

DRAWING NEAR TO CLINK ROAD JUNCTION

With all signals 'off' for the Frome 'cut-off' road, a 'Western' in charge of the down 'Cornish Riviera Express', and travelling at high speed, draws near to the Junction.   1 June 1971.

A memory from the past — a 'pick-up' goods. A 'Hymek' with a short goods — including a gunpowder van next to the engine(!) — heading east from Clink Road Junction.

1 June 1971.

Diesel-hydraulic 'Western' Class No. D1023 *Western Fusilier*, slows as she approaches with a train of coal empties. The signals are 'off' for the road into Frome and at the Junction she will be turning right and then taking the branch up to Radstock. 28 April 1971.

Diesel-hydraulic No. D1011 *Western Thunderer*, approaching rapidly with a down express from Paddington, has the road for the 'Frome cut-off' line.   14 June 1974.

CLINK ROAD JUNCTION

As at Westbury, the Great Western Railway built, in the early 'thirties, a 'cut-off' line to bypass Frome Station and its attendant severe speed restrictions. The junctions at the east and west ends of the 'Frome cut-off' are Clink Road and Blatchbridge respectively.

A stone train from Foster Yeoman's quarry at Merehead, hauled by 'Peak' Class diesel-electric No. 165, comes up the main line and past the Box, travelling at a sedate pace.
12 September 1973.

Brush Type 2 No. D5843, still in the old livery, comes out from Frome with a long train of empty wagons.
12 September 1973.

CLINK ROAD JUNCTION

'Western' Class No. D1041 *Western Prince*, approaching with a down tanker train, has the road for the 'Frome avoiding' line. 12 September 1973.

A few years after the last of the Western Region's diesel-hydraulic 'Warship' Class had been withdrawn from service, BR decided to bestow the names of warships on their Class 50 diesel-electric locomotives. In January 1978, No. 50035 was named *Ark Royal*, and is seen here in October passing Clink Road box at high speed with the 06.31 Penzance to Paddington express.

6 October 1978.

At a much more moderate pace, a 'Peak' trundles down the main line with a train of empty wagons for Merehead Quarry.

14 June 1974.

'Western' Class diesel-hydraulic No. D1023, *Western Fusilier*, with a long train of coal empties, breasts the rise near Mells on the way to Radstock.   28 April 1971.

THE FROME-RADSTOCK BRANCH

Just to the east of Frome Station, a single line branches off to run up to Radstock. Originally it ran through to Bristol, but the Radstock-Bristol section was closed in 1968, and the track lifted.

Diesel-hydraulic 'Warship' Class No. D823, *Hermes*, passes by near Mells with a train of coal from Radstock, bound for Portishead Power Station.   24 February 1971.

A train of wagons hauled by Class 31 No. 31112, on their way to Marcrofts Wagon Works at Radstock for repair. The private line branching off for Whatley Quarry is in the foreground.   10 June 1975.

▼

THE PRIVATE LINE OFF THE FROME-RADSTOCK BRANCH, WHICH RUNS TO WHATLEY QUARRY

'A diesel amidst the daisies' — an SR Class 33 No. 33055 leaves the Radstock branch (which can be seen in the background) and starts on the run up to Whatley Quarry with a train of empty stone wagons.

10 June 1975.

Coming across an impressive bridge on the private line, an SR Class 33 heads towards the Frome branch with a train load of stone from Whatley Quarry.   6 June 1975.

Class 31 No. 31170 standing in the station with a semi-fast down to Weymouth.
13 July 1978.

FROME — STILL WITH A BRUNEL OVERALL ROOF

Early in October 1978 major alterations were made to the track layout at Westbury. Whilst this work was being carried out, Westbury Station was temporarily closed and arrangements were made for all trains normally scheduled to stop there, to call at Frome instead. One of the expresses diverted from the Frome 'cut-off' to call at Frome Station was the 12.30 Paddington to Paignton, seen here 'framed' by the goods shed entrance, setting off for the continuation of her run west, hauled by a Class 50.
6 October 1978.

▲
Early morning on a fine autumn day —
another down diverted express, the 07.30
Paddington to Penzance, sets off again after
her brief stop, hauled by Class 50 No. 50007
Hercules.   6 October 1978.

BLATCHBRIDGE JUNCTION — AT THE WESTERN END OF THE FROME 'CUT-OFF' LINE

On a fine evening in early October, a Class
50 speeds past Blatchbridge Junction with a
down express, having come down the
'Frome avoiding' line.   7 October 1978.

Signalman Adrian Vaughan, now a well-known railway author, on duty in Witham Box. 7 August 1975.

An up express, the 06.35 Penzance to Paddington, hauled by Class 50 No. 50038, passing Witham Box at a rapid pace. 18 July 1975.

WITHAM

A branch leaves the main line here to run up to Cranmore. Before being truncated, this branch ran via Shepton Mallet and Wells, to Yatton where it connected with the main line from Bristol to the West of England via Taunton.

Two miles east of Cranmore, connections are made with the extensive private rail system of Foster Yeoman, which serves this company's vast quarry at Merehead.

A down evening express, the 15.30 Paddington to Penzance, hauled by diesel-hydraulic No. D1057 *Western Chieftain*, passes by the Box at high speed. In the foreground is the branch line which runs up to Cranmore and the vast Merehead Quarry. 8 July 1975.

As a 'Western' Class diesel-hydraulic No. D1015 *Western Champion*, slowly approaches with a train of empty wagons for Merehead Quarry, Driver Robin Gould leans out, ready to be given the token for the single-line branch.
18 July 1975.

ON THE WITHAM-CRANMORE BRANCH

Diesel-hydraulic 'Western' Class No. D1069 *Western Vanguard*, comes steadily up the steep bank with a long train of empty stone wagons bound for Foster Yeoman's Quarry at Merehead. The ruling gradient on the climb up the branch from Witham is 1 in 49.

6 July 1971.

After setting off from the bitumen depot situated at Cranmore, a train of empty bitumen tank wagons in the charge of a diesel-hydraulic 'Hymek', drops cautiously down the branch towards Witham.

14 June 1973.

With storm clouds gathering, *Western Prince* slowly propels a loaded stone train away from the quarry towards the branch. The train is just passing the temporary level crossing over the A361 Frome-Shepton Mallet road, diverted whilst a new road bridge was being built over the new rail connection to the quarry. 14 August 1970.

MEREHEAD QUARRY

In the 1960s, Foster Yeoman, the quarry owners, decided to transfer much of their output from road to rail. So in 1969/70 they had constructed a single line to connect their quarry with the Cranmore branch of British Railways.

On a hazy morning in mid-September, a 'Peak' No. 149, comes cautiously down the branch with a train load of stone. The new East Chord leading into the quarry system is the line on the right hand side. 14 September 1973.

Shortly after the new East Chord had been put in, and the siding accommodation increased substantially, a 'Peak' No. 46008, carried out some test running over the lines to verify that these locomotives were suitable for the new layout.   8 October 1973.

EXTENSIONS TO THE QUARRY RAIL SYSTEM

As a result of a heavy increase in demand, Foster Yeoman developed their rail system considerably, putting in a new line to connect with the branch, so forming an East Chord.

A sullen day of drenching rain in early September 1973, had matured into a glorious autumn evening. Just as the lengthening shadows were stretching out to reach the deep cutting near Studley Farm, a 'Peak' came toiling up the steep bank from Witham with a long train of empty stone wagons for Merehead Quarry.   5 September 1973.

MEREHEAD QUARRY STONE TRAFFIC

Class 47 No. 47068, hauling a train of empty wagons, comes in carefully over the East Chord on the approach to the quarry sidings.   30 September 1974.

'Peak' No. 165 propels a train-load of stone out of the quarries towards the branch. The procedure is for empty wagons to come into the quarry system via the East Chord and full trains are propelled out to the branch, using the original line. This is for safety reasons — with the locomotive at the rear there can be no 'breakaways' running back down into the quarry. (This *did* actually happen one night shortly after the line came into use, but, almost miraculously, no one was hurt.)   14 September 1973.

On Friday, 14 September, an official visit was made by senior BR officers to inspect the new, much enlarged system put in by Foster Yeoman. The 'special' was formed of a manager's saloon coach, hauled by Brush Type 4 No. 1724.   14 September 1973.

STONE TRAFFIC DOWN THE BRANCH FROM MEREHEAD TO THE MAIN LINE AT WITHAM

Having propelled her train out of the quarry and on to the branch, a Class 47 sets off with her stone train for the run down to Witham.
14 June 1973.

Drawing near to the main line — diesel-hydraulic No. D1055 *Western Advocate* with a train-load of stone carried in Foster Yeoman's own wagons.   7 August 1975.

'Peak' No. 46012 arrives at Witham with her stone train, and is held on the branch, for an express to pass, before being allowed out on to the main line.   7 August 1975.

A Class 50, No. 50046 *Ajax*, heading west at high speed with the 11.30 Paddington to Penzance — the down 'Cornish Riviera'.

26 July 1979.

With harvesting just starting, an up express, the 08.38 Penzance to Paddington, hauled by Class 50 No. 50005, *Collingwood*, passes through the beautiful Somerset countryside on her way up to London.
26 July 1979.

THE WESTERN END OF WHITEBALL TUNNEL

A down HST — the 12.25 Paddington to Penzance — travelling very fast, leaves the tunnel and sweeps past the little signal box.

17 May 1980.

An absolutely immaculate Class 50, No. 50028 *Tiger,* coming swiftly down the bank with a Paddington to Paignton express.   17 May 1980.

With the shadows lengthening, the 12.23 Manchester to Paignton, hauled by Class 47 No. 47010, emerges from the tunnel into the evening sunshine.   17 May 1980.

Emerging from one of the short tunnels west of Dawlish, the 09.20 Liverpool to Penzance passes by, hauled by Class 47 No. 47010.

8 May 1979.

With the sea drowning the sound of her approach, the 14.36 Paignton to Leeds express, hauled by 'Peak' No. 46049, suddenly comes into view, round the curve. 8 May 1979.

'PEAKS' ON DAINTON BANK

'Peak' No. 45017 plodding strongly up the bank with the 08.15 Birmingham to Plymouth express.

8 May 1979.

With Stoneycombe Quarry in the background, 'Peak' No. 45028 comes swiftly down the bank, in charge of the 11.10 Plymouth to Manchester express.　　　　8 May 1979.

▲

A ballast train, hauled by Class 50 No. 50049, *Defiance*, emerges slowly from the tunnel, the down 'Distant' signal having been 'on'. 11 May 1979.

THE WEST END OF DAINTON TUNNEL

With the ballast held at the down 'Home' signal, another Class 50, No. 50014 *Warspite*, comes up the bank, heading east with the 08.38 Penzance to Paddington. 11 May 1979.

The 10.30 Paddington to Plymouth, hauled by Class 50 No. 50046 *Ajax*, draws near to Ivybridge.   9 May 1979.

NEAR IVYBRIDGE

A down express passing over Ivybridge Viaduct.   9 May 1979.
▼

SPECIAL TEST TRAINS

Engaged on a high-speed braking test run, one of the HST prototype power cars, hauling a Derby Mobile laboratory car and an HST coach, passes swiftly through Sydney Gardens, Bath, heading east.

9 May 1978.

Two Class 50s on a haulage test, enter the East Chord at Hawkeridge Junction, with a stone train of 3,000 tons.

3 March 1980.

THE ANNUAL WEED KILLING TRAIN

An immaculate Class 31 No. 31317 running slowly through the Limpley Stoke valley with the annual weed-killing train.
11 May 1980.

A glittering SR Type 3, No. D6559 — just out of Eastleigh Works after a general overhaul — comes strongly up the bank with a train of ballast from Whatley Quarry.
14 August 1973.

UPTON SCUDAMORE BANK

Between Westbury and Warminster on the line to Salisbury.

Descending the bank very cautiously, a 'Western' Class diesel-hydraulic, No. D1064 *Western Regent* approaches Westbury with a long train of empty stone wagons. 9 August 1973. ▶

EAST OF WARMINSTER   Diesel-hydraulic 'Hymek', No. D7018, running south-east from Warminster on a cold but clear late autumn afternoon with the Bristol, Temple Meads, to Portsmouth Harbour train.   5 November 1970.

▲

The 13.35 Bristol, Temple Meads to Portsmouth Harbour train hauled by 'Hymek' No. D7013, still in the old two-tone green livery, drawing near to Sherrington on the run to Salisbury.　22 October 1971.

NORTH WEST OF SALISBURY

An SR Type 3 heading north-west from Sherrington with a train of empty ballast wagons bound for Whatley Quarry, near Frome.　16 August 1972.

BUCKHORN WESTON TUNNEL — ON THE OLD SOUTHERN MAIN LINE TO THE WEST OF ENGLAND

Sadly, this magnificent main line is now but a shadow of its former self. After coming under the control of the Western Region west of Salisbury, the line was singled and much of the traffic re-routed to run over former Great Western lines.

On a glorious summer's day, an SR Class 33, No. 33011, emerges from Buckhorn Weston Tunnel with the 10.10 Exeter to Waterloo. 4 June 1974.

The 11.00 down express from Waterloo, hauled by SR Class 33, No. 33033, sweeps down towards Buckhorn Weston Tunnel.   4 June 1974.

SR CLASS 33s ON THE OLD SOUTHERN MAIN LINE WEST OF SALISBURY

Two SR Class 33s, Nos. 33027 and 33042 climbing westwards from Gillingham with the 09.20 Brighton to Exeter express.
17 May 1980.

An up express from Exeter to Waterloo, hauled by an SR Class 33, heads away from Buckhorn Weston Tunnel towards Gillingham.   4 October 1978.

CLASS 47s APPEAR ON DIVERTED STONE TRAINS

Due to engineering work at Westbury, some stone trains from Merehead Quarry which normally ran via Westbury to Salisbury and beyond, were diverted to run west to Castle Cary and then down to Yeovil Junction. Here the engine ran round her train, and then headed east up the Southern line to Salisbury. A Class 47 on one of these diverted stone trains is seen here, climbing away from Buckhorn Weston Tunnel.   4 October 1978.

WESTERN REGION 'WARSHIPS' ON THE OLD SOUTHERN MAIN LINE

After the Southern main line west of Salisbury came under the control of the Western Region, the WR introduced their diesel-hydraulic 'Warships' for working the expresses. However after the diesel-hydraulic 'Warships' had been phased out, the SR Class 33s came back on the scene again until they, in turn, were replaced by the new diesel-electric Class 50s. In this picture, a diesel-hydraulic 'Warship', No. D817 *Foxhound* — still in red livery — is seen approaching Buckhorn Weston Tunnel with the 09.08 down express from Waterloo.   2 June 1971.

The 08.23 (SO) Barnstaple to Waterloo, heading east from Buckhorn Weston Tunnel, hauled by Class 50 No. 50034. In 1978, the Western Region started to name these locomotives after warships, and No. 50034 bears the name *Furious*.   17 May 1980.

THE 'BERKS & HANTS' LINE OF THE OLD GREAT WESTERN — NEARING WOODBOROUGH

The 11.30 from Paddington — the 'Down Riviera' — hauled by a Class 47, draws near to Woodborough.

7 November 1975.

EAST OF GREAT BEDWYN

Class 47 No. 47054, in charge of an up excursion bound for Paddington, speeds eastwards from Great Bedwyn towards Little Bedwyn.   7 September 1975.

PASSING LITTLE BEDWYN

Running beside the Kennet and Avon Canal, a down express, hauled by a diesel-hydraulic 'Western', passes the pretty village of Little Bedwyn.   7 September 1975.

NEAR HUNGERFORD A Class 50 No. 50012 *Benbow*, in charge of a down express, draws near to Hungerford.
12 May 1980.

THE ADVANTAGE OF RAIL TRAVEL

Shortly after dawn on a bitterly cold morning — with patches of mist and 'black ice' on the roads — an HST sweeps past Claverton Weir on its way from Bristol to London. Inside, its passengers sit back in complete comfort and totally at ease.   17 December 1978.

Of course, the alternative would have been to drive to London up the M4, but in what sort of a state would you have arrived after a nerve-racking journey?

On a horrible, wet, winter's night, an HST stops gently in Bath Station, just 69 minutes after leaving Paddington. Again, the passengers have had a smooth, relaxed journey without a care in the world.   26 October 1980.

Or perhaps you would have preferred to 'battle' down the M4 in the dark and in torrential rain? Half-blinded by great sheets of spray thrown out by huge lorries travelling at high speed. Pulling out to overtake — and praying that the road ahead was clear? *And* taking twice as long over your journey?

THE TAIL ENDS

The trailing power car of a Paddington-bound HST, accelerating away from Bath, passes by the trailing power car of a down HST from Paddington, just about to leave Bath for Bristol.

10 May 1978.